The Art of Falling

for Chris

The Art of Falling

Kim Moore

SEREN

Seren is the book imprint of
Poetry Wales Press Ltd.
57 Nolton Street, Bridgend, Wales, CF31 3AE
www.serenbooks.com
facebook.com/SerenBooks
twitter@SerenBooks

The right of Kim Moore to be identified as
the author of this work has been asserted in accordance
with the Copyright, Designs and Patents Act, 1988.

ISBN: 978-1-78172-237-4
e-book: 978-1-78172-239-8
Kindle: 978-1-78172-238-1

A CIP record for this title is available from the British Library.

The publisher acknowledges the financial assistance of the Welsh Books Council.

Book Cover Painting by Nicholas Stedman.

Printed in Bembo by Bell & Bain Ltd, Glasgow

Author blog: https://kimmoorepoet.wordpress.com/blog/

Contents

I

II

How I Abandoned My Body To His Keeping

III

I

And the Soul

And the soul, if she is to know
herself, must look into the soul…
             – Plato

And the soul, if she is to know herself
must look into the soul and find
what kind of beast is hiding.

And if it be a horse, open up the gate
and let it run. And if it be a rabbit
give it sand dunes to disappear in.

And if it be a swan, create a mirror image,
give it water. And if it be a badger
grow a sloping woodland in your heart.

And if it be a tick, let the blood flow
until it's sated. And if it be a fish
there must be a river and a mountain.

And if it be a cat, find some people
to ignore, but if it be a wolf,
you'll know from its restless way

of moving, if it be a wolf,
throw back your head
and let it howl.

My People

I come from people who swear without realising they're swearing.
I come from scaffolders and plasterers and shoemakers and carers,
the type of carers paid pence per minute to visit an old lady's house.
Some of my people have been inside a prison. Sometimes I tilt
towards them and see myself reflected back. If they were from
Yorkshire, which they're not, but if they were, they would have been
the ones on the pickets shouting *scab* and throwing bricks at policemen.
I come from a line of women who get married twice. I come from
a line of women who bring up children and men who go to work.
If I knew who my people were, in the time before women
were allowed to work, they were probably the women who were
working anyway. If I knew who my people were before women
got the vote, they would not have cared about the vote. There are
many arguments among my people. Nobody likes everybody.
In the time of slavery my people would have had them if they
were the type of people who could afford them, which they
probably weren't. In the time of casual racism, some of my people
would and will join in. Some of my people know everybody
who lives on their street. They are the type of people who will argue
with the teacher if their child has detention. The women
of my people are wolves and we talk to the moon in our sleep.

Boxer

If I could make it happen backwards
so you could start again I would,
beginning with you on the floor,
the doctor in slow motion
reversing from the ring, the screams
of the crowd pulled back in their throats,
your coach, arms outstretched, retreats
to the corner as men get down from chairs
and tables, and you rise again, so tall,
standing in that stillness in the seconds
before you fell, and the other girl, the fighter,
watch her arm move around and away
from your jaw, and your mother rises
from her knees, her hands still shaking,
as the second round unravels itself
and instead of moving forward,
as your little Irish coach told you to,
you move away, back into the corner,
where he takes your mouth guard out
as gently as if you were his own.
The water flies like magic from your mouth
and back into the bottle and the first round
is in reverse, your punches unrolling
to the start of the fight, when the sound
of the bell this time will stop you dancing
as you meet in the middle, where you come
and touch gloves and whisper good luck
and you dance to your corners again,
your eyes fixed on each other as the song
you chose to walk into sings itself back
to its opening chords and your coach
unwraps your head from the headguard,
unfastens your gloves, and you're out
of the ring, with your groin guard,
your breast protector, you're striding
round that room full of men,
a warrior even before you went in.

A Psalm for the Scaffolders

who balanced like tightrope walkers,
who could run up the bracing
faster than you or I could climb
a ladder, who wore red shorts
and worked bare-chested,
who cut their safety vests in half,
a psalm for the scaffolders
and their vans, their steel
toe-capped boots, their coffee mugs,
a psalm for those who learnt
to put up a scaffold standing
on just one board, a psalm
for the scaffolder who could put
a six-inch nail in a piece of wood
with just his palm, a psalm
for those who don't like rules
or things taking too long, who now
mustn't go to work uncovered,
who mustn't cut their safety vests
or climb without ladders, who must
use three boards at all times,
a psalm for the scaffolders
who fall with a harness on,
who have ten minutes to be rescued,
a psalm for the scaffolder who fell
in a clear area, a tube giving way,
that long slow fall, a psalm for him,
who fell thirty feet and survived,
a psalm for the scaffolder
who saw him fall, a psalm for those
at the top of buildings, the wind whistling
in their ears, the sky in their voices,
for those who lift and carry
and shout and swear, for those
who can recite the lengths of boards
and tubes like a song, a psalm for them,
the ones who don't like heights
but spent their whole life hiding it,
a psalm for those who work too long,
a psalm for my father, a psalm for him.

Teaching the Trumpet

I say: imagine you are drinking a glass of air.
Let the coldness hit the back of your throat.

Raise your shoulders to your ears, now let
them be. Get your cheeks to grip your teeth.

Imagine you are spitting tea leaves
from your tongue to start each note

so each one becomes the beginning of a word.
Sing the note inside your head then match it.

At home lie on the floor and pile books
on your stomach to check your breathing.

Or try and pin paper to the wall just by blowing.
I say: remember the man who played so loud

he burst a blood vessel in his eye? This was
because he was drunk, although I don't tell

them that, I say it was because he was young,
and full of himself, and far away from home.

The Trumpet Teacher's Curse

A curse on the children who tap the mouthpiece
with the heel of their hand to make a popping sound,
who drop the trumpet on the floor then laugh,
a darker curse on those who fall with a trumpet
in their hands and selfishly save themselves,
a curse on the boy who dropped a pencil
on the bell of his trombone to see if it did
what I said it would, a curse on the girl
who stuffed a pompom down her cornet
and then said it was her invisible friend who did it,
a curse on the class teacher who sits at the back
of the room and does her paperwork,
a curse on the teacher who says *I'm rubbish at music*
in a loud enough voice for the whole class to hear,
a curse on the father who coated his daughter's trumpet valves
with Vaseline because he thought it was the thing to do,
a curse on the boy who threw up in his baritone
as if it was his own personal bucket.
Let them be plagued with the urge to practise
every day without improvement, let them play
in concerts each weekend which involve marching
and outdoors and coldness, let their family be forced
to give up their Saturdays listening to bad music
in village halls or spend their Sundays at the bandstand,
them, one dog and the drunk who slept there the night before
taking up the one and only bench, Gods, let it rain.

The Messiah, St Bees Priory

Today, everywhere is covered in snow
and the priory is a huge mouth
swallowing the cold, as if the snow
has come to dispel all memory
of that day in June, the sudden heat of it,
the constant call of sirens.

I was standing on a hill in Barrow,
looking over the water to Millom,
knowing the police cars rushing past
would be too late. The roads
that brought the gunman there
would stop them finding him –

Askam, Broughton, Ravenglass
and all the tops of Corney Fell between
and people cutting hedges, riding bikes,
who hadn't heard the news, who
would stop and help a passing driver
without thinking.

Today, November snow makes us
more inclined to sit together,
the violins gathered round a heater,
the breath of singers caught in air,
the audience, still in hats and coats
and scarves, huddle closer

then lean forward as I call the dead
to listen. They are singing *Hallelujah*
to forget that afternoon when the sun
was a hand on the backs of their necks,
when villages, hardly talked about before
were the names on everybody's lips.

Hartley Street Spiritualist Church

The first hymn is Abba: *I Believe in Angels.*
No music because Jean has forgotten the tape.
We sing without, led from the front by a medium
with long red hair, who announces that a dog
is in the room, and is, at this very moment,
sitting next to the tea urn. This means someone

is ready to be healed. Another medium stands,
running coloured ribbons through her hands,
points behind and says a woman is pacing
up and down, flicking her hair and pouting,
and will anyone claim her, does anyone
have a relative who would do such a thing?

And then the psychic artist stands up, unrolls
a scroll, a picture he drew many years ago,
in anticipation of this day, a man in a flat cap
with a cigarette, a man who used to get back
from work and watch the sun go down
from his back porch and smoke and smoke,

and he says *this is your Grandad isn't it*
to a woman who nods vigorously
and then he starts to draw an old lady
with short hair who he says is standing
next to me, and am I feeling warm
because this is the energy of Spirit

and do I ever feel I'm being followed
even though there's no one there,
because this is the energy of Spirit,
and come to think of it, I think I am warm
but that might be because everybody's
staring, and he's whispering, over

and over, *it's your Grandma isn't it*
and I believe him, I want to think she's there,
even though in his drawing she has permed hair
and glasses. He gives me the image
of this woman. Later on I bin it, but before
we go we sing *I Believe in Angels* again.

Tuesday at Wetherspoons

All the men have comb-overs,
bellies like cakes just baked,
risen to roundness. The women tilt
on their chairs, laughter faked,

like mugs about to fall, cheekbones
sharp as sadness. When the men
stand together, head for the bar
like cattle, I don't understand

why a woman reaches across, unfolds
his napkin, arranges his knife and fork
to either side of his plate. They're all
doing it, arranging, organising, all talk

stopped until the men, oblivious,
return. My feet slide towards a man
with one hand between his thighs,
patience in his eyes who says *you can*

learn to love me, ketchup
on the hand that cups my chin,
ketchup around his mouth,
now hardening on my skin.

In Praise of Arguing

And the vacuum cleaner flew
down the stairs like a song
and the hiking boots
launched themselves
along the landing.

And one half of the house
hated the other half
and the blinds wound
themselves around
each other.

And the doors flung
themselves into the street
and flounced away
and the washing gathered
in corners and sulked.

And the bed collapsed
and was held up by books
and the walls developed
scars and it was a glorious,
glorious year.

Barrow To Sheffield

Even though the train is usually full of people
I don't like, who play music obnoxiously loud
or talk into their phones and tell the whole carriage
and their mother how they're afraid of dying
even though they're only twenty-five,

even though the fluorescent lights
and the dark outside make my face look like
a dinner plate, even though it's always cold
around my ankles and there's chewing gum
stuck to the table and the guard is rude

and bashes me with his ticket box,
even though the toilet smells like nothing
will ever be clean again, even though
the voice that announces the stations
says *Bancaster* instead of *Lancaster*,

still I love the train, its sheer unstoppability,
its relentless pressing on, and the way the track
stretches its limb across the estuary
as the sheep eat greedily at the salty grass,
and thinking that if the sheep aren't rounded up

will they stand and let the tide come in, because
that's what sheep do, they don't save themselves,
and knowing people have drowned out there
like the father who rang the coast guard,
who put his son on his shoulders as the water rose

past his knees and waist and chest, the coast guard
who tried to find him, but the fog came down,
and though he could hear the road, he didn't know
which way to turn, but in a train, there are no choices,
just one direction, one decision you must stick to.

This morning the sun came up in Bolton and all the sky was red and a man in a suit fell asleep and dribbled on my shoulder till the trolley came and rattled in his ear and he woke up and shouted *I've got to find the sword.*

Sometimes You Think of Bowness

and swans on the pier being fed by hand
and the ice cream shop with twenty-six flavours
and the wooden rowing boats like slippers

and how Windermere is one place and Bowness
another, and just a stretch of road joins them
together, of the hotel on the hill, the Belsfield

and Schneider, walking down to take the steamer,
his butler following with breakfast on a silver tray,
but mostly you think of the people, drawn to water,

and how it looks in the rain, as if the shops
were made of water, of ducking into a doorway
and carrying the smell of rain inside.

I'm Thinking of My Father

I'm thinking of my father in the backyard
throwing more and more wood on the fire.
The slow dusk of summer descends
and he's throwing more wood on the fire

as his brother lies dying, but then I think
aren't we all dying, but he knows,
my uncle, he knows what will kill him,
a tumour the size of a fist and growing.

Still my father throws wood on the fire
as the new cherry blossom tree waits
to be planted, he throws wood on the fire,
while my mother sits alone and watches TV

and outside the fire gets higher. My father
cuts wood with a saw that screams as if someone
is dying and he doesn't care about splinters
or safety as long as the fire gets higher.

All the stone lions and grave little gnomes
in their cheerful red breeches are waiting
and the lamp that's addicted to heat
flickers on, flickers off and the lawn sits

in its shadows and dark and its falsehoods
and the ending begins with its terrible face,
its strange way of being, its short way of living
and my father stops throwing wood on the fire.

After Work

I walk the dogs as dusk begins
its slow descent between the trees,
the drift of leaves, the greyness in the air

and if there was a moment
when I thought the body was a cage,
I knew it then, watching the rooks

take their message to the sky,
how everything is changing
but you and I, we keep going,

you on your path, me on mine,
constant as the railway line
ticking itself to sleep.

Here is the loneliness of November
and its failure at an ending, this light
that takes us out of sync each time,

the Christmas tree put up too early,
and the words that don't begin.
Where are my words in November?

They scatter with the call of geese
unseen above low-lying clouds.
Look at the trees and how

they've dropped every thought
they had to earth, and the poor horse
in his field, slanted at a crazy angle

to the sky, the way he rubs his neck
against the fence post and shudders,
what must he think of you and I?

That Summer

Whatever went wrong that summer
started with the redwings that fell from the sky
in a country no one could remember the name of.

I watched the trails of planes and realised
you had a redwing in your chest instead of a heart.

The dragonflies were tiny bottles whirring around
our heads. Knowing about the redwing didn't help.

On television the towers were whole, then they fell,
then they were whole again. I knew you were in
New York, that this would change you.

I said *Come back and find me someday*
but the music was so loud and the next day
I moved countries and forgot to tell you.

There are no dragonflies here of course.
They froze in mid-air and sounded like spoons
on a flagstone floor as they dropped.

What does this mean? Nothing really,
except I knew you, then I didn't, then I stopped.

All My Thoughts

I didn't take your face between my hands
like a cup filled to the brim with water
or trace the outline of your shoulders
or learn the grace of each separate part.

I learnt nothing of your language,
but watched your glasses steam up
as you passed from street to pub
then slowly clear again, two ghosts

disintegrating on the lens. I didn't
walk the edges of the sea, or learn
how a border shifts like smoke,
only knew you, wrapped inside your coat.

We stood, my forehead pressed against
your chest, your hand stroking my hair.
I couldn't look at you or speak,
you whispered *tell me, tell me* and this

felt like a forgotten hurt, your lips
on mine, while the birds of my thoughts
wheeled overhead and the life (the life
I knew) called to me in sadness

open, let me in and so I did. I watched
you go and all the wolves and all
the stars went with you and I
walked back, back across the bridge.

The Art of Falling

This is for falling which is so close to failing
or to falter or fill; as in *I faltered when I heard
you were here*; as in *I filtered you out
of my life*; as in *I've had my fill of falling*:
a fall from grace, a fall from God,
to fall in love or to fall through the gap,
snow fall, rain fall, falling stars,
the house falls into disrepair,
to fall in with the wrong crowd,
to fall out of love, to fall like Jessica
who fell down a well and watched
the bright disc of the sun and moon
slowly passing, for twins who start
so close together they must fall
apart for the rest of their lives
or be damned, to fall down a hill
like a brother, to follow like a sister,
to be a field and fall fallow, to fall pregnant,
for vertigo, the cousin of falling,
for towers and stairs and pavements
which are the agents of falling,
for the white clifftop of a bed,
for climbers and roofers and gymnasts,
for the correct way to fall,
loose-limbed and floppy,
to fall apart after death,
for ropes and fences and locks
which carry the act of falling inside,
for fall which over the ocean
means Autumn, which means leaves
like coins of different colours
dropped from the pockets of trees,
which means darker evenings,
which means walks with the dogs,
which means walking alone
and not falling apart at the sound
of your name, which God
help me, sounds like falling.

II

How I Abandoned My Body To His Keeping

In That Year

And in that year my body was a pillar of smoke
and even his hands could not hold me.

And in that year my mind was an empty table
and he laid his thoughts down like dishes of plenty.

And in that year my heart was the old monument,
the folly, and no use could be found for it.

And in that year my tongue spoke the language
of insects and not even my father knew me.

And in that year I waited for the horses
but they only shifted their feet in the darkness.

And in that year I imagined a vain thing;
I believed that the world would come for me.

And in that year I gave up on all the things
I was promised and left myself to sadness.

And then that year lay down like a path
and I walked it, I walked it, I walk it.

Body, Remember

Body, remember that night you pretended
it was a film, you had a soundtrack running
through your head, don't lie to me body,
you know what it is. You're keeping it from me,
the stretched white sheets of a bed,
the spinning round of it, the high whining sound
in the head. Body, you remember how it felt,
surely, surely. You're lying to me. Show me
how to recognise the glint in the eye of the dog,
the rabid dog. Remind me, O body, of the way
he moved when he drank, that dangerous silence.
Let me feel how I let my eyes drop, birds falling
from a sky, how my heart was a field, and there
was a dog, loose in the field, it was worrying
the sheep, they were running and then
they were still. O body, let me remember
what it was to have a field in my chest,
O body, let me recognise the dog.

He was the Forgotten Thing

He was the forgotten thing, the blackened tree
that doesn't grow, that doesn't fall, he was
the car that wouldn't pull over, the tide coming in,
he was everything I put my heart against,
the low set and turn of heads when he entered a room,
he was buses roaring past like blind heroes,
he was stolen things. He was the connecting parts
of train carriages, he was windows with curtains
to keep out the street, he was a car that drove
through the night, he was a fist not an eye, he was
an eye not an ear, he had thoughts that took over
the day like weather, like the rain coming in,
he was nothing I thought of, he was not
what was promised, he was walking home
through the snow with his arm like a curse
round my neck, he was not black and white,
he was nothing like that. And look at him now,
standing in a field surrounded by crows, one arm
pointing north but his face to the west,
he knows to be still with his black button eyes,
his stitched-on smile. The birds have come
to pull out the straw that keeps him upright.
Look how they carry him home in their
sharp little beaks once again.

When I Was a Thing With Feathers

When I turned mimic and could sing only what I'd heard
a hundred times before, when my throat changed shape
and left me unable to articulate the edges of words,
when feathers pierced my skin growing from within,
when I tried to let my head fall to my hands and found
only wings, when I was able to fly but chose never
to stutter from tree to earth and back again, when I
could live on almost nothing, when I saw myself reflected
in windows, my eyes like tiny stones and my beak
the smallest sword, when I knew fear was just a thing
to be bargained with, inside my feathered heart
was another feathered thing, born white but slowly
turning black, the way the crow in all the stories
was turned black for speaking truth.

Followed

It fell all day and cut off each street.
Nothing worked the way it was
supposed to. Cars abandoned
at the sides of roads. The snow
with a silent, insistent will of its own.
People in suits hurried past,
smiling despite themselves,
despite being late, snowlight
on their faces, opened up
at the slow speed of moving.
The traffic lights flashed
red/amber/green and every bus
brought shuddering to its knees.
In that quiet light he looked
taller than in the morning
when I left, everything black
about him, his coat and shoes
and trousers, his hands and heart
and eyes. How pleased
he was to see me, his arm heavy
on my shoulders. The smell
of his leather coat filled my nose
and took the cold away.
I told myself it was just a dog I heard,
that night on the street
when all I could see was snow.
I almost turned but then I followed.
I followed to the darkness of our home.

The Knowing

The story goes that the light slipped past/and entered the room like a shout/he stood over me/a woodcutter entered the forest/and the trees began to warn each other/it was July or maybe June/the knowing settled at my throat/a clever raven/it never left/does not believe in trees or flying/the light slipping past/it is sometimes painful/to have a knowing at your throat/that clever raven/but better than the alternative/something small and bruised/the raven knows most things/it remembers nothing/this is really about the trees/which saw it all.

The Language of Insects

This is the language of insects, this body
low to the ground, this single purpose,
this living with dirt, this stop-start-stop,
this construction of fabulous structures,
this non-human logic, this cannot-live-without-
the-other, this no-good-as-a-single-entity,
this language, this language, please I cannot
meet your kind again, you showed me
what knees were really for, no forgiveness,
none at all, this movement, this movement,
there are spiders that eat one another,
there are ants that follow each other
in a spiral, smaller and smaller
until they take the life from one another,
a black fist, all I know creeps to the edges
of rooms, the flies on the windowsills,
the buzzing, the buzzing that made it begin.

When Someone is Singing

When someone is singing the old carols –
the earth hard as iron, snow on snow,
when cold brings the world to silence,
when the name of the city we lived in is spoken,
when lorries are parked in lines at service stations,
when making a decision, when another year ends,
when a coach ticks to itself in the heat,
when I see a couple arguing in public,
when I hear someone shouting or swearing,
when I see boats or think of the sea,
when I remember I know how someone can break,
if somebody spits on the pavement, if somebody spits,
when I stand at a bus stop, when I visit the doctors,
when I get in a car with someone else driving,
when I see bouncers in nightclub doorways,
with the taking and giving of pain, when I'm afraid,
it's only then I think of him, or remember his name.

Your Hands

I can't remember your fingernails
but I remember the quick movement

of your hands, how you rolled each
cigarette, your tongue licking the paper.

For months I found brown twists
of tobacco in the creases of clothes,

filters in their plastic sleeves
or delicate papers spread like wings.

I can't remember a single thing we said
to one another but I remember your

black leather jacket, your one pair
of good black trousers. I remember

arguing all night, but not what about.
I remember sleep was something

that did not belong to me. I swear
I remember nothing, just your outline

at the foot of the bed, you are shouting
as if calling me from some distant shore,

but there's no such thing as sound,
no such thing as shore.

On Eyes

That we are not born with tears
but learn them in the passing of a month.
That a black eye can be caused by a tennis ball,
a fist or a door. That blue-eyed people
share a common ancestor with every
other blue-eyed person in the world.
That there are microscopic creatures
living in our eyelashes. That these
will not speak up for us. That a black
eye fades from dark-blue to violet
to yellow-green. That dolphins sleep
with one eye open. That on seeing
danger, the eye will close. That we
do not enter this world with colour.
That it takes only a few days for
a black eye to heal. That the eye
is the fastest moving part of the body
but not the fastest healing for that
is the tongue. That to avoid a black eye
make sure rugs and carpets are well placed
and there are no wrinkles in your floor.
Scorpions have twelve eyes.
Worms have no eyes at all.
To avoid a black eye, always wear
protective gear, such as a helmet or goggles.

Your Name

Because they tried to make me say your name,
the shame and blame and frame of it,
the dirty little game of it, the dark and distant
heart of it, the cannot be a part of it,
the bringing back the taste of it till I was changed
inside the flame of it, the cut and slap and shut
of it, the rut and fuck and muck of it,
the not-forgotten hurt of it, the syllable
stop-dead of it, the starting in the throat of it,
the ending at the teeth of it.

Encounter

It was you, the set of your shoulders, your way
of standing, your arms folded across your chest,

your belly a small hill, it was you, it was you,
your hair dark and shaved, your skin brown

from the sun. I turned on my heel and went
back into the classroom and sank to my knees

behind the door and I prayed you away,
to a God I'd never spoken to before,

I wished you away like a child. I looked again
and again through the darkened glass,

it was you, but it was not you. Your soul
had entered this man, his eyes and his hands

were yours, it was you, I could swear it
on anything you named, if I stopped looking

it would always be you. So I looked
and I looked till my eyes burned from

not blinking and I watched him walk away.
Your soul left his body as if it had

never been there at all and all that was left
of you was a taste of smoke in the air.

I Know

I know this bus stop, the green and flaking paint of it.
I know this road I have to cross, I know the traffic
rushing past. I know these seven steps. I know
this door, its weight, its tone as it speaks in anger.
I know this hallway, the hexagon tiles, red and black
and red and black. I know this second door.
I know what it is for the body to open one door
then the other while the heart stays silent.
I know these floorboards. I know what it is
to lie here, the body like a boat, caught by its heels
in a harbour. I know what it is to kneel here
as if in prayer, if prayers were ever full of tears.
Ten years on, it's almost heady to look back,
see myself kneeling on the floor, watching
the hysterical skittering of the phone.
His voice, trapped and low: *pick up the phone.*
You'd better pick up the fucking phone.
I know the top of my head, I know my shoulders,
can see how everything I knew is scattered
across the floor, like love and all the weight of it.
I know this room. I know that sofa, the orange of it,
its patient waiting. I know how it feels to walk
backwards into it. I know this place. I leave my self
down there, kneeling, still alone.

Translation

Don't we all have a little Echo in us, our voices stolen,
only able to repeat what has already been said:
you made me do it he says and we call back *do it, do it.*

Wouldn't any of us, if pushed, sit on the riverbank
and comb snakes from our hair, or think that in our grief
we could become a sea bird, our outstretched bodies

like a cross nailed to the wind? Who amongst us
hasn't sat astride a man more bull than man
as he knelt in the dirt, for no good reason we can speak of?

There was a time when I was translated by violence,
there were times I prayed to be turned into a flower
or a tree, something he wouldn't recognise as me.

The World's Smallest Man

Today I make you into the world's smallest man.
You are so small I open my hand and you dance
on the great landscape of my palm.

You are a thin stick of a man. When you stretch out
along my life line, your feet touch my wrist
and your head rests below my index finger.

You are a small man, but like a small dog
you are unaware of your size. Sometimes
you go missing for days then jump out

and shout *surprise!* But you do not mean surprise.
I decide to make you even smaller, the size
of an insect. Now you can walk upside down.

I think of all the places I could leave you
now you are smaller than the lightest
water boatman, but you keep shrinking

till you are less than a grain of salt,
so small you are living on my skin.
And, once I breathe, I breathe you in.

How I Abandoned My Body To His Keeping

What happened sits in my heart like a stone.
You told me I'd be writing about it
all my life, when I asked
how to stop saying these things to the moon.
I told you how writing it makes the dark
lift and then settle again like a flock of birds.

You said that thinking of the past like birds
who circle each year will make the stone
in my chest heavy, that the dark
that settles inside me will pass. You say it
is over, you say that even the moon
can't know all of what happened, that to ask

to forget is to miss the point. I should ask
to remember. I should open myself to the birds
who sing for their lives. I should tell the moon
how his skin was like smoke, his hand a stone
that fell from a great height. It
was not what I deserved. The year was dark

because he was there and my eyes were dark
and I fell to not speaking. If I asked
him to leave he would smile. Nothing in it
was sacred. And I didn't look up. The birds
could have fallen from the sky like stones
and I wouldn't have noticed. The moon

was there that night in the snow. The moon
was waiting the day the dark
crept into my mouth and left me stone
silent, stone dumb, when all I could ask
was for him to *stop, please stop.* The birds
fled to the trees and stayed there. It

wasn't their fault. It was nobody's fault. It
happened because I was still. The moon
sung something he couldn't hear. The bird
in my heart silent for a year in the dark.
This is the way it is now, asking
for nothing but to forget his name, a stone

that I carry. It cools in my mouth in the dark
and the moon sails on overhead. You ask
about birds, but all I can talk of is stones.

Human

I imagine you reading about yourself
in the safety of your car, parked for the night,
the engine silent, the motorway sings, the filth
of driving for many miles has settled right

into your skin. You've eaten the cheap
food and the cheap coffee in the roadside café,
you're ready to put the seats down and sleep
the moon away. Your hands – your hands are steady.

It doesn't feel as if ten years have passed.
I remember the bedroom window. The truck
parked and blocking all the light. I could laugh
if this thing in my chest stopped breaking. It was luck

that got me out of it. Still I want you to read these words.
I try to make you human. I pretend that I've been heard.

III

Red Man's Way

When I finally get here and see the channel
with the tide out and the boats drowning

in sand, and the gulls calling overhead,
sometimes hassling a lone crow from the sky

and the old path across the channel
as if someone has drawn a finger

across the mud to make it so, I feel full,
as if one person can't carry this with them

and be unchanged, as if I could speak seagull
and they would come, cursing, articulate,

their wings the colour of sky, as if I could
put my hand up and stop the noise of traffic

from the nearby road, or pinch out the lights
from the shipyard with my finger and thumb

and it's never silent here, because the wind
likes to run its hands over and over the land,

shaping the newly planted trees to strange angles,
as slowly, year by year, the bank covers itself

with grass, and last summer, for the first time,
ox-eye daisies, tall as your knees and fearless.

If We Could Speak Like Wolves

If I could wait for weeks for the slightest change
in you, then each day hurt you in a dozen
different ways, bite heart-shaped chunks
of flesh from your thighs to test if you flinch
or if you could be trusted to endure,

if I could rub my scent along your shins to make
you mine, if a mistake could be followed
by instant retribution and end with you
rolling over to expose the stubble and grace
of your throat, if it could be forgotten

the moment the wind changed, if my eyes
could sharpen to yellow, if we journeyed
each night for miles, taking it in turns
to lead, if we could know by smell
what we are born to, if before we met

we sent our lonely howls across the estuary
where in the fading light wader birds stiffen
and take to the air, then we could agree
a role for each of us, more complicated
than alpha, more simple than marriage.

Candles

after C.P. Cavafy

How fast the line of cold, dead candles grows.
Look how they put their wax heads in their hands
to weep, or fold themselves chest first towards
the floor, caught at the end of some performance.

How soon they lose their height, how soon
the black smoke rises, stopping their slow slide
along the edges of each other. They nosed
their way towards the ground with the certainty

of saints, threw the shadows of our hearts against
the walls. Now I see dead candles everywhere,
haunted by their last breath, their single-minded
need to burn again, to soften themselves, to ache

towards each other. Paused in this last act of falling,
they do not want to hold themselves together.

Picnic on Stickle Pike

You say you don't want me to describe
the couple we saw, halfway up Stickle Pike,
the woman dipping her head
to the man's white belly, his penis
lolling like a Labrador's tongue.

I try instead, to write about our picnic,
the brown blanket you carried from the car,
how you marched about, identifying flowers,
spying with your binoculars on a fire engine
crawling over Birker Fell.

And what about the view, you say, we can see
Scafell and Crinkle Crags and Harter Fell
and the sun is out, and the wind farm is waving
but I'm thinking about that couple,
middle-aged, embarrassed,

hiding their faces in each other's tight embrace
as we walked past, but before they noticed us
the woman was a long-necked bird, bending
its proud neck to feed, and the man lay
like an expensive table.

The Fall

Last weekend I fell in love with the bathroom,
its clean white tiles, the towels hanging like flags
in a tiny hot country, this place that caught you,
that stopped you falling from the earth.

Blank-faced, it tells no tales, won't give up
the secret of how you went from standing
to stretched across the floor, your feet
at its northern border, your head to the south,

your eyes rolling, wild as a horse, your body
an empty house abandoned to the wind and rain.
When I lift your head, there's no resistance.
It moves like water at the bottom of a tilted bowl.

Was it my shouting that made you surface?
Slowly, slowly you returned, the bath (faithful
creature) in the same position as when you left,
the sounds you made so far from words.

You brought another language back with you,
the hotel quiet as a church, you didn't know
the body you were in was yours, blood leaked
from your mouth and gathered on your chin,

the sink and toilet impassive and standing guard.
You remembered nothing of your journey,
minutes of your life deleted and only this room
to witness your passing. I can only guess

which loving object tried to catch you, which voice
pulled me from my sleep. I kick the bath. It answers
in a low familiar tone. I stamp. The floor bellows
its reply. The room beneath echoes like a drum.

The Dead Tree

How easy it is to love the dead tree,
despite not knowing its kind,
its branches spread against the sky.
Even in death it reaches upward,
before the left hand turn,
after the shortcut across the moor.
In winter, in the fog,
sheep lie on the road for warmth
until the car is close enough
to breathe on them
and then they straighten their legs
and clatter away like coat hangers.
It's easy to think that nobody
has been this way for years.
This is the right time, eight
or nine at night. The workers
from Sellafield already home,
they have forgotten the sea
and the beach of stones
in the bright light of home.
Today, someone has left a mattress
miles from the nearest town,
on the corner of the switchback,
half-folded on its side,
a woman posing for a painting.
A farmer raises one index finger
less than half an inch
to acknowledge you,
mistaking you for someone
who belongs here,
because of the time of night,
because you don't use your brakes
to slow the car down, just
the natural camber of the road,
he doesn't know you're only
here for the tree, he'd think you mad
but how many things does he know

that never change, shouldn't this be
a tourist spot with a myth of its own:
Here is the tree, struck by lightning
five terrible times and it survived
until the last, when it dropped
every leaf it had and would ever have
down to the ground in fright.
Maybe some part of it fell like he did
and its soul jumped from its wood and fled
and its trunk and each branch
turned white in shock,
but its poor tree soul, only used
to moving in the wind or hunching
its shoulders against rain or snow,
so used to being tree-shaped,
feeling rooted all through the earth,
the tree soul couldn't find its way back
so it jumped into the nearest living thing.
Someone is changing their mind
with the seasons, someone is losing
everything then finding it again.
Somebody is walking around
with a tree soul inside them.

How Wolves Change Rivers

By singing to the moon, when the beavers move in, by the growing of trees, when the soil resists the rain, when the sky rubs its belly on the leaves, by singing to the wind, by killing the deer, by moving them on from the valleys, by the birds coming back to the trees, by singing to the water, with the return of the fish, with the great ambition of beavers, with the return of bears moving across the land like dry ships, by an abundance of berries, by the bear reaching and pulling down branches, by the green coming back, by the green coming back, by the steadiness of soil, by the deer leaving the valley and the gorges, by the aspen growing, by the cottonwood growing, by the willow growing, by the songbirds singing to the trees, by the beavers coming back to love the trees, by the absence of coyotes and the abundance of rabbits, by the bald eagle and the raven who arrive to minister to the dead, by the glove of a weasel and the burn of the fox, by the gathering of pools, the holding together of the river bank by the trees, by the river finding its spine once again.

Some People

Some people cannot be helped or saved or changed
some people   some people would stand out in the rain
and drown if they could some people   some people
have never seen the stars and that is all you can say
about them some people   some people are made hard
by life and don't realise they're shouting some people
some people like to tell others what to do some people
some people would walk into the cannons every day
of their lives some people   some people get lost
and then stay lost some people   some people
aren't around even when they're around some people
some people can't control their minds some people
can't control their fists some people   some people
like to pretend they're in a film some people
some people don't come from this century some people
don't exist   some people think they're being helpful
some people   some people say they're going to be honest
some people   some people should have been born
to someone else some people   some people think
they were born to apologise some people   some people
carry something that isn't theirs all their lives some people
some people think some people

How the Stones Fell

after Ovid

We learnt that we were born from stones, that the last
man and woman to survive the flood climbed from their raft
onto the shoulders of a mountain and looked across the water
which had swallowed everything.

For days there had been a sea but no shore, now as the water
curled back its lip and let go of the tops of trees
the man and woman followed, walking down the slope,
their feet touching the edges of the water,

their arms full of the bones of the earth, their hair long
and flowing to their waists. They cast stones behind them
and from the hand of the man a stone fell and grew into
another man and from the hand of the woman

a stone fell and grew into another woman and so we grew,
our eyes like flints and our mouths tasting of the earth.
We were born from stones and we were destined to live
like stones, warming ourselves in the sun,

cracking when the temperature fell, we said there was
something of the sea in us, but in this, like many other things
we lied, it was never water in our hearts, we carried stones
in our pockets, we carried them in our hands.

A Room of One's Own

Give her strength as she sits beside the river,
in that city she didn't name, in October,
the leaves around her burning red and purple,
the bridge staring only at its secret self
under the water. Give her strength
when she's turned away from the library
or walks on the grass and gets chased off,
as the thought she almost had gasps for breath,
give her strength to push the life back in it,
to follow it through the city streets to the museum,
where more books about women live
than on any other subject in the world.

Give her strength to see an answer,
she'll need as much as Atlas needs,
his shoulders curved under the loneliness
of holding up the world. Give her strength
when that strange wind blows and the bricks
glow like fire and the world conspires
to blind her with beauty, to make her calm,
accepting. Give her strength to follow
the thought they tell her not to have.

And let her move through me,
my curved fingers pressed against
the tattooist's belly as he writes
her words in my skin. I'm ashamed,
I'm biting my lip while he talks of immigrants
and the deserving poor, like old people,
like his ma, and who would I rather
give money to, as if that's the only choice.
I'm biting my lip while her words
and the flame of their birth set in.
I'm biting my lip, he's not a cruel
or even a stupid man, give me strength
to count, keep track of such days as these,
how many times I stay calm, say nothing.

The Master Engraver

Let me tell you about a man called Graham Short
who can engrave the Lord's Prayer on the head
of a pin, who cut the Motto *Nothing Is Impossible*
on the edge of a razor blade, who wrote the names
of the thirty-eight England World Cup scorers
on the bottom of a football stud, who waits
to make a single stroke between heartbeats,
who works so slowly, so quietly, that when
the mice come, their footsteps cause a tremor
that can obliterate several words. Watch him
late at night, when the lorries don't run,
his solitary light shining for as long as the dark
holds the city to account. This is the way
to slow down time. Sometimes, he says,
he thinks he's made it stop, his engraving arm
bound with a luggage strap so only his fingertips
are free to move, his stethoscope now warming
on his chest, his resting heartbeat thirty beats a minute,
his skin stretched tight. This is his covenant,
his ritual, this working through the night.

Suffragette

And if you saw her hiding in the air ducts of Parliament
it was only to listen to the speeches.

And if she set fire to post boxes and burnt letters,
it was only certain envelopes she put pepper in.

And if she threw a rock or two, at one carriage
or another, they were, at least, wrapped in words:

rebellion against tyrants is obedience to God.
And if, being imprisoned, her and a thousand like her

went on hunger strike, at least no one died:
The Cat and Mouse Act of 1913

sent the starving women out on licence,
and brought them back when they were well again.

And if an angry guard forced a hose inside her cell
and filled it with water, at least she didn't drown.

And if she hid in a cupboard in the House of Commons
the night of the census it was only to claim it

as her official residence. And if her friends delivered
themselves as human letters to Downing Street,

but were sent back, unopened, at least they made
the news. And, not knowing whether she chose

to die or whether in her dreams, she saw the king's horse
flying through the line, her sash around its neck,

at least we know of the bruised shins of the horse,
of the jockey, 'haunted by that woman's face.'

John Lennon

He called the local churchyard the bone orchard,
imitated the choir master by conducting the cats,
stole fruit from the church at harvest time,
called kissing his uncle *giving squeakers*,
read Alice in Wonderland over and over,
shaped like a hairpin, legs propped against a wall.

His Aunt Mimi said *the guitar's all very well*
John, but you'll never earn your living with it,
brought him up to speak proper, to write
thank you letters, was outraged at his hair.
Rolf Harris said being angry with him was like
trying to punch away a raincloud.

When the Beatles played in New York, not even
a hubcap was reported stolen. He was born
without brakes, this boy who wouldn't wear
his glasses, who dreamt each night of climbing
in a plane above Liverpool, circling higher
and higher until the city disappeared from view.

Shelley

Packing his case wasn't easy – his mother
matching socks he'd left strewn around the room –
his father piling sets of science books, thinking

at last there'd be a respite from the mischief-making,
the experiments with cats in thunderstorms,
the fire balloons and his constant questions *why*

such a thing behaved in such a way. He's bouncing
on the seat as the carriage pulls away, his moon-face
looking back at them, gaze so intent they can't help

but turn around. There's nothing there, just
the house stretching its shadow across the lawn.
He's smiling, mouth twitching in a silent prayer

(his mother reassures herself) but no, he's counting
down the seconds until the device he's left inside
the chimney is ready to explode and puff great breaths

of smoke in every room. He's on his way to blow up
his school desk and a hundred-year-old oak, to elope
to Ireland and scatter pamphlets, flinging them

from the windows of his lodgings, or stuffing them
in passing carriages. He presses his nose to the glass,
laughs to see their eyes wide as crockery,

the red in his father's face as he shakes a fist
and runs for the house, his mother, turning
like a horse, hiking her skirts to her knees.

Wallace Hartley

When he was found, still in his uniform,
his violin strapped to his back, people began
to remember the way he'd played each night,
not just the last, the dip and turn of his shoulders
as he led the orchestra through a waltz,
how the ship was all lit up and smiling
like a brand new town, those nights before
the boats were counted, when the chink of cutlery
was louder than the band, how he played on
as boys kicked chunks of ice across the deck
when the ship was immense and black
against a sky full of flares and stars.

Chet Baker

The night before his death, he sat at the window
of the Hotel Prins Hendrik, one knee pulled
to his chest, the other leg dangling inside the room
and this was how he dropped like a stone,
he was playing his flugel, softly, alone, one long
drawn-out cry and he lost his balance

halfway through the century. He was alone.
We were all alone, nobody could believe
he would fall so carelessly, from Room 210
of all places, of all things, to fall from a window
into the dark of morning, to let the years hang
so heavy on his skin, to rebuild his embouchure

from nothing and then to be undone, we didn't
lower ourselves from the height of winter
to the depths of Autumn, we were watching
from the snow we came from, his face
the grey of November, his eyes two leaves
of slowly changing colour.

Dear Mr Gove

dear Mr Gove today I taught the children not to sit like bags of small potatoes in their chairs I taught them how to breathe with their bellies like babies do when they are sleeping we pretended we were balloons of different colours filling up with air dear Mr Gove we played *long note beat that* we looked up who holds the world record for the longest note it was a clarinet player who managed to play for one minute and thirteen seconds without taking a breath we held our notes as if we were monks singing a drone in a cathedral where the roof rises like a giant wing against the sky dear Mr Gove today the whole class played hot cross buns we talked about the great height of the note E we held thin blue straws between our lips and some of us went on to play an E and some of us fell towards a low A with its ledger line hovering above it and another piercing its poor head dear Mr Gove we are brilliant at trying some of us know what crotchets and minims are and we will know this all our lives but some of us still call them black and white notes we make up sayings to help us read like Elephants Go Bananas Doing Flips like Electric Green Brains Dance Forever we play the riff to Eye of The Tiger and sing along in the voices of tigers if tigers had voices like ours today Mrs Johnson forgot how to play a D and Harry told her which valves to press I do not know how to measure this Mr Gove please send help and there is also the problem of Matthew who cannot read or write too well but who can play Mary Had A Little Lamb with perfect pitch there is the problem of his smile afterwards and how we write this down today we watched the muppets singing Bohemian Rhapsody for no good reason other than that it was fun and while I am confessing small transgressions last week we watched Mr Bean play an invisible drum kit the children have been playing an invisible drum kit in the playground dear Mr Gove I did not stop them today we talked about the muscles in the lip and tongue we did not know we had control of so many muscles we tried to look like musicians Mr Gove please help us

In Another Life

For Jan Glas

I think that in another life, I must have known you –
maybe we were brothers who loved or hated one another
or maybe we were neighbours destined to grow old together
or strangers who nod hello when passing in the street
or maybe one of us was a king, and the other in the army
and on a routine inspection our eyes just met
or maybe we were soldiers who would die for one another,
maybe we were the last two speakers of a minority language,
maybe I was a farm animal and you were a fair-haired farmhand,
maybe we ran away to America together, or maybe we
were miners and loved our yellow canaries, maybe you
were the canary and I felt your heart beating on my palm,
maybe you were a nurse and I was your favourite patient,
maybe we were buried on a hill, standing side by side.

Give Me a Childhood

after John Burnside

Give me a childhood and I will live
as owls do. On those long journeys south
by car, I will fly next to the window
on white silent wings. I will wear my heart
as a face. Each time I speak it will be a question.

Sometimes I'll turn the hinge of my neck
to look at my body, staring out from the dark
of the car, while my soul swoops under bridges,
over train lines. Somewhere, at the far edge
of the day, my mother will call to me.

She's making shoes again, the part that
covers the top of the foot, the piece of foot
that never does the thing a foot was born
to do. This is called interlacing. This is why
her hands are cracked, her nails bitten shy.

I can put on the heavy garments of the soul.
I can tether myself to the earth if I choose.
the cats eyes, set into the road with what
I think of as love. The same songs, over and over.
The world non-existent beyond the headlights.

New Year's Eve

This one started the same as the others,
the waiting for midnight, talking to strangers
as what's left of the year drags itself off

and we stand on the bridge as fireworks
burst silent at midnight, the tipping point
when you could fall between years

and no one would notice, but afterwards
it wasn't the same, because we danced to
'Not Alone Anymore' by the Travelling Wilburys

and I believed him, Roy Orbison, I mean,
I remember sitting at my grandmother's feet
with his voice on repeat,

and this time was different because David
was in love, as if love hadn't happened before,
as if he'd been months at sea and just returned

and this was the last thing they had to do this year.
They've not learnt to be disappointed in one another
as the year that they met skulks from the room

and the new one comes in with its arms full of love,
the dogs smelling of rain and the woods
where we walked the last dusk of the year

and who else would know the words to Alanis
but David, who fell asleep sitting up, swaying
like a paper boat on slow moving water.

Notes and Acknowledgements

Acknowledgements are due to the Editors of the following publications where these poems, or earlier versions of them, first appeared:

Acumen; Dark Mountain, Firecrane; Magma; Mslexia; Newspaper Taxis: Poems after the Beatles (Seren); *New Welsh Review; Poem; Poetry London; Poetry News; Poetry Review; Poetry Wales; The Lampeter Review; The National Humanist; The North; The Ofi Press; The Rialto; Sculpted: Poetry of the North West; Times Literary Supplement.* A number of these poems also appeared in a pamphlet 'If We Could Speak Like Wolves' (Smith/Doorstop).

'A Psalm For The Scaffolders' was commended in the 2013 Troubadour Poetry Competition. 'Hartley Street Spiritualist Church' was a runner up in the 2012 Kent and Sussex Poetry Competition. A version of 'The Art of Falling' won 2nd place in the 2013 Buzzwords Poetry Competition.

'All My Thoughts' is a response to a Strauss song, with text by Felix Ludwig Julius Dahn and was set to music by the composer Gemma Balmoody to be performed as part of the Strauss Celebration Season at the Bridgewater Hall in Manchester.

'On Eyes': much of the information from this poem comes from the websites http://medicalnewstoday.com and www.lenstore.co.uk

'In Another Life' was inspired by 'The Fair-Haired Farmhand' by Jan Glas.

This collection was written with the help of an Eric Gregory Award in 2010 and a New Writing North award in 2014.

I would like to thank my friends at the Poetry Business Writing School, Brewery Poets and Barrow Writers who read and commented on many of these poems. Thanks also to David Tait, David Borrott, Noel Williams, John Foggin, Clare Shaw, Jennifer Copley, Mike Barlow, Carola Luther, Andrew Forster at the Wordsworth Trust and my Editor Amy Wack, for all of their help and encouragement.